HOME SCHOOL MATH

1st Grade
Addition Problems

{TIMED TEST}

HOMESCHOOL
WORKBOOKS

1.	1	2.	2	3.	9	4.	2	5.	7
	+ 9		+ 6		+ 7		+ 9		+ 6

6.	0	7.	1	8.	3	9.	0	10.	7
	+ 2		+ 8		+ 0		+ 3		+ 3

11.	5	12.	6	13.	7	14.	2	15.	3
	+ 3		+ 2		+ 0		+ 4		+ 10

16.	0	17.	9	18.	2	19.	9	20.	8
	+ 2		+ 7		+ 8		+ 7		+ 4

21.	2	22.	5	23.	2	24.	6	25.	10
	+ 4		+ 9		+ 3		+ 10		+ 0

26.	2	27.	10	28.	0	29.	6	30.	10
	+ 7		+ 6		+ 7		+ 5		+ 3

31.	3	32.	8	33.	10	34.	1	35.	6
	+ 3		+ 8		+ 1		+ 0		+ 7

36.	9	37.	7	38.	1	39.	9	40.	0
	+ 9		+ 0		+ 2		+ 5		+ 4

41.	9	42.	3	43.	0	44.	6	45.	0
	+ 5		+ 6		+ 1		+ 4		+ 0

1. 2 + 6	**2.** 7 + 3	**3.** 8 + 9	**4.** 1 + 0	**5.** 4 + 5
6. 0 + 1	**7.** 0 + 1	**8.** 9 + 9	**9.** 4 + 2	**10.** 6 + 8
11. 4 + 5	**12.** 0 + 3	**13.** 2 + 4	**14.** 2 + 7	**15.** 3 + 9
16. 8 + 2	**17.** 0 + 9	**18.** 7 + 1	**19.** 3 + 10	**20.** 1 + 3
21. 3 + 10	**22.** 2 + 1	**23.** 0 + 9	**24.** 8 + 3	**25.** 2 + 10
26. 2 + 3	**27.** 3 + 5	**28.** 6 + 7	**29.** 9 + 2	**30.** 8 + 4
31. 1 + 6	**32.** 2 + 4	**33.** 7 + 4	**34.** 3 + 7	**35.** 5 + 8
36. 10 + 10	**37.** 0 + 10	**38.** 10 + 6	**39.** 6 + 8	**40.** 8 + 2
41. 8 + 8	**42.** 8 + 10	**43.** 5 + 0	**44.** 4 + 7	**45.** 1 + 1

1. 4 + 7	**2.** 4 + 7	**3.** 4 + 4	**4.** 5 + 7	**5.** 6 + 0
6. 4 + 6	**7.** 5 + 3	**8.** 6 + 9	**9.** 4 + 0	**10.** 6 + 0
11. 9 + 0	**12.** 3 + 3	**13.** 2 + 4	**14.** 10 + 9	**15.** 6 + 5
16. 6 + 2	**17.** 8 + 3	**18.** 7 + 10	**19.** 8 + 10	**20.** 0 + 5
21. 5 + 9	**22.** 8 + 10	**23.** 1 + 10	**24.** 8 + 10	**25.** 9 + 7
26. 6 + 3	**27.** 4 + 5	**28.** 5 + 8	**29.** 2 + 9	**30.** 9 + 8
31. 8 + 6	**32.** 1 + 9	**33.** 2 + 10	**34.** 9 + 4	**35.** 9 + 10
36. 1 + 0	**37.** 9 + 8	**38.** 3 + 4	**39.** 9 + 8	**40.** 1 + 3
41. 8 + 8	**42.** 0 + 4	**43.** 3 + 3	**44.** 0 + 10	**45.** 7 + 10

1. 1 + 10	2. 6 + 4	3. 6 + 9	4. 0 + 5	5. 9 + 1
6. 8 + 5	7. 8 + 6	8. 2 + 6	9. 10 + 9	10. 10 + 9
11. 4 + 2	12. 2 + 4	13. 4 + 2	14. 7 + 4	15. 5 + 4
16. 2 + 9	17. 7 + 7	18. 9 + 7	19. 2 + 6	20. 10 + 6
21. 1 + 9	22. 2 + 6	23. 6 + 4	24. 7 + 4	25. 0 + 0
26. 5 + 0	27. 9 + 2	28. 8 + 5	29. 0 + 1	30. 2 + 7
31. 9 + 2	32. 0 + 1	33. 7 + 4	34. 9 + 8	35. 10 + 8
36. 0 + 6	37. 2 + 7	38. 4 + 1	39. 4 + 10	40. 9 + 7
41. 3 + 4	42. 4 + 8	43. 3 + 5	44. 8 + 2	45. 2 + 5

1. 1	2. 2	3. 6	4. 0	5. 9
+ 4	+ 4	+ 9	+ 5	+ 6

6. 2	7. 2	8. 0	9. 2	10. 8
+ 9	+ 7	+ 8	+ 4	+ 7

11. 1	12. 3	13. 0	14. 5	15. 2
+ 7	+ 10	+ 9	+ 3	+ 2

16. 8	17. 2	18. 4	19. 1	20. 1
+ 10	+ 2	+ 10	+ 5	+ 1

21. 10	22. 3	23. 10	24. 4	25. 4
+ 9	+ 7	+ 6	+ 6	+ 10

26. 2	27. 2	28. 7	29. 6	30. 10
+ 6	+ 5	+ 8	+ 5	+ 3

31. 2	32. 4	33. 4	34. 0	35. 8
+ 2	+ 1	+ 4	+ 4	+ 6

36. 7	37. 2	38. 8	39. 0	40. 3
+ 1	+ 1	+ 8	+ 10	+ 2

41. 9	42. 4	43. 5	44. 9	45. 1
+ 6	+ 0	+ 3	+ 7	+ 7

Name_____ Date _____ Score _____

1. 3
+ 2

2. 0
+ 8

3. 7
+ 0

4. 3
+ 6

5. 4
+ 7

6. 8
+ 10

7. 3
+ 5

8. 3
+ 6

9. 9
+ 8

10. 10
+ 1

11. 2
+ 9

12. 4
+ 2

13. 5
+ 2

14. 0
+ 2

15. 1
+ 8

16. 0
+ 4

17. 10
+ 4

18. 8
+ 6

19. 4
+ 1

20. 1
+ 3

21. 8
+ 10

22. 5
+ 10

23. 6
+ 5

24. 8
+ 8

25. 6
+ 4

26. 8
+ 5

27. 1
+ 5

28. 9
+ 1

29. 8
+ 7

30. 1
+ 6

31. 5
+ 2

32. 10
+ 1

33. 8
+ 8

34. 5
+ 7

35. 4
+ 9

36. 4
+ 7

37. 3
+ 0

38. 9
+ 3

39. 4
+ 4

40. 6
+ 0

41. 6
+ 6

42. 6
+ 3

43. 1
+ 5

44. 9
+ 10

45. 5
+ 10

6

1.	10 + 3	2.	3 + 5	3.	10 + 6	4.	8 + 4	5.	1 + 2
6.	3 + 8	7.	1 + 9	8.	0 + 8	9.	3 + 1	10.	7 + 10
11.	0 + 10	12.	1 + 9	13.	9 + 4	14.	10 + 7	15.	5 + 2
16.	7 + 6	17.	3 + 6	18.	0 + 7	19.	1 + 9	20.	8 + 8
21.	1 + 2	22.	6 + 10	23.	6 + 4	24.	9 + 5	25.	9 + 8
26.	7 + 7	27.	3 + 4	28.	4 + 2	29.	8 + 9	30.	0 + 2
31.	6 + 10	32.	9 + 9	33.	10 + 5	34.	10 + 3	35.	2 + 5
36.	6 + 9	37.	6 + 2	38.	2 + 9	39.	9 + 9	40.	6 + 8
41.	1 + 7	42.	0 + 0	43.	5 + 6	44.	4 + 10	45.	2 + 1

1. 8 + 5	2. 5 + 7	3. 1 + 10	4. 9 + 6	5. 3 + 9
6. 3 + 6	7. 5 + 7	8. 1 + 8	9. 7 + 4	10. 5 + 0
11. 0 + 6	12. 1 + 4	13. 0 + 10	14. 7 + 7	15. 10 + 10
16. 7 + 2	17. 7 + 6	18. 8 + 9	19. 9 + 1	20. 9 + 9
21. 8 + 8	22. 7 + 9	23. 4 + 9	24. 7 + 5	25. 5 + 7
26. 4 + 1	27. 3 + 4	28. 9 + 8	29. 10 + 6	30. 4 + 1
31. 8 + 7	32. 0 + 9	33. 5 + 0	34. 6 + 2	35. 7 + 6
36. 0 + 4	37. 7 + 10	38. 9 + 2	39. 6 + 0	40. 3 + 7
41. 5 + 7	42. 8 + 4	43. 8 + 6	44. 9 + 4	45. 7 + 0

Name_____ Date _____ Score _____

1. 4 + 9	2. 2 + 10	3. 9 + 7	4. 9 + 2	5. 5 + 10
6. 4 + 1	7. 7 + 9	8. 6 + 1	9. 0 + 5	10. 1 + 1
11. 8 + 0	12. 3 + 10	13. 9 + 5	14. 4 + 8	15. 8 + 0
16. 1 + 5	17. 5 + 0	18. 1 + 6	19. 9 + 5	20. 3 + 6
21. 10 + 6	22. 2 + 6	23. 1 + 0	24. 0 + 3	25. 4 + 3
26. 0 + 4	27. 10 + 4	28. 3 + 9	29. 10 + 2	30. 10 + 6
31. 9 + 5	32. 4 + 9	33. 7 + 1	34. 9 + 0	35. 3 + 3
36. 1 + 9	37. 0 + 5	38. 7 + 3	39. 5 + 5	40. 0 + 6
41. 8 + 3	42. 4 + 6	43. 4 + 10	44. 8 + 2	45. 4 + 2

1. 2 + 1	**2.** 5 + 5	**3.** 9 + 10	**4.** 3 + 2	**5.** 9 + 6
6. 1 + 0	**7.** 5 + 1	**8.** 10 + 4	**9.** 10 + 8	**10.** 4 + 3
11. 0 + 8	**12.** 3 + 10	**13.** 6 + 9	**14.** 7 + 5	**15.** 9 + 0
16. 4 + 2	**17.** 9 + 0	**18.** 1 + 0	**19.** 3 + 4	**20.** 4 + 1
21. 10 + 7	**22.** 6 + 8	**23.** 8 + 2	**24.** 3 + 4	**25.** 7 + 2
26. 8 + 0	**27.** 3 + 4	**28.** 10 + 10	**29.** 8 + 8	**30.** 9 + 8
31. 6 + 10	**32.** 0 + 5	**33.** 6 + 3	**34.** 10 + 2	**35.** 1 + 6
36. 9 + 6	**37.** 1 + 2	**38.** 9 + 8	**39.** 0 + 6	**40.** 3 + 8
41. 2 + 8	**42.** 4 + 6	**43.** 4 + 2	**44.** 10 + 7	**45.** 0 + 10

1. 6
  + 8
  ___

2. 8
  + 1
  ___

3. 9
  + 3
  ___

4. 4
  + 0
  ___

5. 1
  + 6
  ___

6. 5
  + 5
  ___

7. 7
  + 8
  ___

8. 7
  + 2
  ___

9. 9
  + 6
  ___

10. 1
  + 1
  ___

11. 3
  + 6
  ___

12. 10
  + 4
  ___

13. 5
  + 2
  ___

14. 9
  + 10
  ___

15. 7
  + 9
  ___

16. 4
  + 5
  ___

17. 7
  + 10
  ___

18. 10
  + 1
  ___

19. 0
  + 5
  ___

20. 4
  + 4
  ___

21. 8
  + 5
  ___

22. 8
  + 5
  ___

23. 1
  + 0
  ___

24. 0
  + 7
  ___

25. 9
  + 4
  ___

26. 6
  + 2
  ___

27. 8
  + 5
  ___

28. 6
  + 7
  ___

29. 6
  + 9
  ___

30. 10
  + 8
  ___

31. 5
  + 5
  ___

32. 5
  + 5
  ___

33. 5
  + 8
  ___

34. 8
  + 1
  ___

35. 9
  + 5
  ___

36. 3
  + 8
  ___

37. 7
  + 1
  ___

38. 10
  + 5
  ___

39. 0
  + 10
  ___

40. 7
  + 9
  ___

41. 0
  + 4
  ___

42. 0
  + 6
  ___

43. 1
  + 3
  ___

44. 0
  + 9
  ___

45. 4
  + 5
  ___

1. 10
  + 2
  _____

2. 9
  + 7
  _____

3. 5
  + 8
  _____

4.   4
  + 10
  _____

5. 3
  + 5
  _____

6. 9
  + 0
  _____

7. 2
  + 5
  _____

8. 4
  + 0
  _____

9. 3
  + 5
  _____

10. 2
  + 2
  _____

11. 5
  + 9
  _____

12. 8
  + 4
  _____

13. 3
  + 2
  _____

14. 7
  + 7
  _____

15. 10
  + 1
  _____

16. 9
  + 3
  _____

17. 7
  + 1
  _____

18. 6
  + 8
  _____

19.   3
  + 10
  _____

20. 1
  + 0
  _____

21. 1
  + 2
  _____

22. 8
  + 5
  _____

23. 10
  + 6
  _____

24. 7
  + 1
  _____

25. 9
  + 8
  _____

26. 4
  + 5
  _____

27. 7
  + 3
  _____

28. 1
  + 5
  _____

29. 10
  + 1
  _____

30. 7
  + 6
  _____

31. 0
  + 6
  _____

32. 1
  + 8
  _____

33. 8
  + 6
  _____

34. 10
  + 3
  _____

35. 8
  + 4
  _____

36. 10
  + 1
  _____

37. 6
  + 9
  _____

38. 4
  + 3
  _____

39. 8
  + 1
  _____

40. 6
  + 1
  _____

41. 0
  + 5
  _____

42. 1
  + 4
  _____

43. 8
  + 6
  _____

44. 3
  + 7
  _____

45. 8
  + 7
  _____

1. 7 + 4	**2.** 2 + 7	**3.** 9 + 4	**4.** 6 + 10	**5.** 5 + 4
6. 9 + 7	**7.** 1 + 8	**8.** 5 + 8	**9.** 6 + 7	**10.** 5 + 2
11. 7 + 0	**12.** 2 + 5	**13.** 3 + 10	**14.** 2 + 3	**15.** 9 + 10
16. 3 + 3	**17.** 2 + 4	**18.** 9 + 8	**19.** 4 + 9	**20.** 3 + 2
21. 4 + 2	**22.** 4 + 3	**23.** 3 + 10	**24.** 2 + 2	**25.** 7 + 5
26. 10 + 6	**27.** 3 + 9	**28.** 6 + 3	**29.** 3 + 1	**30.** 8 + 5
31. 1 + 8	**32.** 0 + 6	**33.** 6 + 3	**34.** 9 + 3	**35.** 3 + 8
36. 5 + 3	**37.** 2 + 6	**38.** 5 + 9	**39.** 10 + 9	**40.** 2 + 2
41. 10 + 6	**42.** 2 + 3	**43.** 2 + 1	**44.** 2 + 7	**45.** 1 + 1

1. 2 + 6	**2.** 3 + 10	**3.** 2 + 9	**4.** 6 + 4	**5.** 4 + 7
6. 9 + 3	**7.** 3 + 2	**8.** 6 + 4	**9.** 10 + 5	**10.** 2 + 8
11. 4 + 4	**12.** 7 + 4	**13.** 7 + 1	**14.** 9 + 4	**15.** 10 + 8
16. 4 + 5	**17.** 3 + 1	**18.** 0 + 4	**19.** 8 + 6	**20.** 10 + 2
21. 6 + 0	**22.** 0 + 6	**23.** 2 + 6	**24.** 10 + 8	**25.** 10 + 5
26. 3 + 6	**27.** 2 + 2	**28.** 1 + 2	**29.** 9 + 1	**30.** 10 + 5
31. 10 + 7	**32.** 10 + 7	**33.** 10 + 10	**34.** 9 + 0	**35.** 2 + 10
36. 1 + 10	**37.** 5 + 0	**38.** 3 + 1	**39.** 4 + 8	**40.** 8 + 3
41. 2 + 7	**42.** 4 + 10	**43.** 6 + 10	**44.** 5 + 10	**45.** 3 + 5

1. 3
    + 0
    ____

2. 5
    + 2
    ____

3. 1
    + 6
    ____

4. 0
    + 10
    ____

5. 7
    + 2
    ____

6. 9
    + 1
    ____

7. 8
    + 3
    ____

8. 3
    + 4
    ____

9. 4
    + 0
    ____

10. 4
    + 6
    ____

11. 0
    + 2
    ____

12. 8
    + 3
    ____

13. 3
    + 7
    ____

14. 5
    + 4
    ____

15. 9
    + 5
    ____

16. 8
    + 6
    ____

17. 10
    + 1
    ____

18. 2
    + 10
    ____

19. 3
    + 2
    ____

20. 0
    + 9
    ____

21. 9
    + 0
    ____

22. 6
    + 2
    ____

23. 9
    + 9
    ____

24. 10
    + 10
    ____

25. 2
    + 5
    ____

26. 8
    + 5
    ____

27. 1
    + 5
    ____

28. 8
    + 4
    ____

29. 1
    + 0
    ____

30. 7
    + 4
    ____

31. 10
    + 5
    ____

32. 6
    + 1
    ____

33. 1
    + 3
    ____

34. 10
    + 10
    ____

35. 1
    + 9
    ____

36. 4
    + 6
    ____

37. 2
    + 3
    ____

38. 5
    + 7
    ____

39. 2
    + 9
    ____

40. 6
    + 5
    ____

41. 0
    + 0
    ____

42. 0
    + 2
    ____

43. 10
    + 4
    ____

44. 4
    + 0
    ____

45. 2
    + 10
    ____

1. 7 + 2	**2.** 4 + 4	**3.** 5 + 2	**4.** 0 + 5	**5.** 7 + 0
6. 4 + 10	**7.** 8 + 9	**8.** 1 + 9	**9.** 7 + 1	**10.** 0 + 4
11. 0 + 5	**12.** 10 + 10	**13.** 2 + 7	**14.** 3 + 1	**15.** 4 + 7
16. 6 + 0	**17.** 3 + 5	**18.** 5 + 0	**19.** 0 + 3	**20.** 9 + 4
21. 10 + 8	**22.** 10 + 3	**23.** 6 + 1	**24.** 3 + 8	**25.** 10 + 3
26. 0 + 4	**27.** 8 + 7	**28.** 10 + 8	**29.** 7 + 4	**30.** 8 + 10
31. 7 + 6	**32.** 0 + 8	**33.** 9 + 4	**34.** 10 + 0	**35.** 1 + 7
36. 2 + 2	**37.** 2 + 7	**38.** 10 + 1	**39.** 9 + 9	**40.** 9 + 2
41. 8 + 0	**42.** 7 + 3	**43.** 0 + 4	**44.** 5 + 8	**45.** 3 + 3

1. 5 + 1 0	2. 0 + 2	3. 4 + 1 0	4. 8 + 4	5. 6 + 3
6. 4 + 6	7. 7 + 7	8. 8 + 3	9. 3 + 1 0	10. 1 + 9
11. 0 + 7	12. 8 + 1	13. 6 + 3	14. 4 + 7	15. 5 + 5
16. 3 + 0	17. 2 + 1	18. 5 + 9	19. 1 + 1 0	20. 2 + 1
21. 8 + 4	22. 8 + 4	23. 1 + 0	24. 9 + 5	25. 2 + 3
26. 6 + 7	27. 8 + 1	28. 0 + 4	29. 2 + 0	30. 3 + 4
31. 3 + 6	32. 0 + 1 0	33. 9 + 4	34. 4 + 1 0	35. 9 + 5
36. 4 + 6	37. 9 + 8	38. 1 + 9	39. 0 + 1 0	40. 1 + 6
41. 3 + 3	42. 2 + 1 0	43. 9 + 3	44. 8 + 4	45. 4 + 8

1. 7 + 3	**2.** 9 + 4	**3.** 10 + 1	**4.** 10 + 10	**5.** 4 + 3
6. 9 + 0	**7.** 3 + 10	**8.** 7 + 3	**9.** 7 + 2	**10.** 8 + 8
11. 0 + 7	**12.** 5 + 4	**13.** 5 + 10	**14.** 5 + 8	**15.** 9 + 1
16. 5 + 1	**17.** 9 + 7	**18.** 4 + 7	**19.** 9 + 1	**20.** 0 + 2
21. 4 + 2	**22.** 2 + 3	**23.** 1 + 2	**24.** 7 + 0	**25.** 5 + 0
26. 1 + 6	**27.** 0 + 2	**28.** 3 + 6	**29.** 2 + 9	**30.** 2 + 0
31. 1 + 3	**32.** 9 + 0	**33.** 8 + 0	**34.** 7 + 0	**35.** 2 + 6
36. 5 + 4	**37.** 10 + 5	**38.** 9 + 5	**39.** 1 + 8	**40.** 3 + 6
41. 9 + 3	**42.** 5 + 4	**43.** 7 + 0	**44.** 10 + 3	**45.** 10 + 8

Name_____ Date _____ Score _____

1. 6 + 5	2. 10 + 5	3. 8 + 5	4. 0 + 8	5. 0 + 4
6. 0 + 9	7. 9 + 8	8. 3 + 8	9. 3 + 9	10. 7 + 1
11. 7 + 4	12. 4 + 2	13. 3 + 10	14. 2 + 4	15. 2 + 7
16. 10 + 8	17. 7 + 1	18. 5 + 8	19. 10 + 3	20. 9 + 0
21. 3 + 8	22. 6 + 8	23. 3 + 0	24. 0 + 7	25. 4 + 10
26. 6 + 10	27. 10 + 9	28. 4 + 7	29. 2 + 5	30. 10 + 8
31. 8 + 7	32. 3 + 6	33. 1 + 10	34. 5 + 0	35. 8 + 4
36. 2 + 9	37. 7 + 9	38. 9 + 7	39. 1 + 9	40. 5 + 7
41. 5 + 2	42. 10 + 7	43. 1 + 4	44. 7 + 2	45. 8 + 3

1. 5 + 9	2. 7 + 5	3. 4 + 0	4. 9 + 10	5. 4 + 3
6. 10 + 10	7. 6 + 2	8. 2 + 7	9. 5 + 5	10. 8 + 10
11. 1 + 0	12. 7 + 5	13. 6 + 2	14. 0 + 1	15. 4 + 2
16. 9 + 2	17. 6 + 3	18. 1 + 3	19. 9 + 5	20. 3 + 0
21. 10 + 0	22. 6 + 10	23. 10 + 1	24. 0 + 1	25. 8 + 1
26. 9 + 7	27. 5 + 10	28. 2 + 0	29. 2 + 9	30. 0 + 8
31. 10 + 3	32. 7 + 10	33. 0 + 2	34. 5 + 3	35. 0 + 7
36. 2 + 7	37. 7 + 5	38. 3 + 7	39. 9 + 5	40. 7 + 10
41. 0 + 10	42. 7 + 5	43. 6 + 10	44. 5 + 0	45. 9 + 1

1. 6 + 0	**2.** 1 + 1	**3.** 4 + 3	**4.** 1 + 2	**5.** 8 + 7
6. 5 + 8	**7.** 7 + 2	**8.** 4 + 5	**9.** 1 + 10	**10.** 8 + 9
11. 0 + 2	**12.** 5 + 0	**13.** 6 + 2	**14.** 8 + 9	**15.** 10 + 10
16. 7 + 7	**17.** 0 + 0	**18.** 7 + 5	**19.** 2 + 10	**20.** 0 + 8
21. 10 + 4	**22.** 3 + 6	**23.** 7 + 5	**24.** 3 + 3	**25.** 6 + 4
26. 6 + 5	**27.** 2 + 6	**28.** 7 + 7	**29.** 0 + 8	**30.** 0 + 8
31. 8 + 10	**32.** 4 + 5	**33.** 3 + 8	**34.** 2 + 4	**35.** 3 + 8
36. 1 + 8	**37.** 6 + 5	**38.** 4 + 5	**39.** 2 + 5	**40.** 0 + 1
41. 0 + 7	**42.** 4 + 2	**43.** 4 + 10	**44.** 3 + 10	**45.** 0 + 10

1. 1 + 5	**2.** 10 + 5	**3.** 10 + 0	**4.** 2 + 4	**5.** 2 + 0
6. 6 + 3	**7.** 2 + 6	**8.** 1 + 8	**9.** 0 + 0	**10.** 0 + 6
11. 7 + 5	**12.** 4 + 6	**13.** 3 + 2	**14.** 10 + 3	**15.** 2 + 3
16. 0 + 5	**17.** 4 + 2	**18.** 9 + 10	**19.** 8 + 8	**20.** 5 + 0
21. 4 + 6	**22.** 10 + 2	**23.** 10 + 1	**24.** 1 + 7	**25.** 8 + 3
26. 8 + 6	**27.** 1 + 2	**28.** 3 + 9	**29.** 9 + 0	**30.** 8 + 9
31. 9 + 4	**32.** 2 + 9	**33.** 10 + 4	**34.** 8 + 9	**35.** 5 + 2
36. 6 + 4	**37.** 8 + 8	**38.** 0 + 1	**39.** 9 + 3	**40.** 9 + 5
41. 3 + 0	**42.** 7 + 9	**43.** 0 + 3	**44.** 3 + 9	**45.** 5 + 7

1. 9 + 9	2. 2 + 2	3. 9 + 8	4. 4 + 2	5. 3 + 8
6. 5 + 7	7. 6 + 9	8. 5 + 7	9. 8 + 3	10. 9 + 3
11. 6 + 6	12. 0 + 3	13. 2 + 1	14. 5 + 2	15. 10 + 10
16. 6 + 0	17. 4 + 2	18. 5 + 3	19. 5 + 8	20. 4 + 10
21. 5 + 2	22. 2 + 9	23. 9 + 7	24. 4 + 6	25. 1 + 6
26. 3 + 3	27. 9 + 3	28. 2 + 8	29. 3 + 7	30. 5 + 5
31. 1 + 9	32. 9 + 6	33. 6 + 5	34. 7 + 3	35. 4 + 4
36. 0 + 10	37. 2 + 9	38. 10 + 6	39. 10 + 7	40. 8 + 2
41. 9 + 1	42. 9 + 3	43. 10 + 9	44. 8 + 8	45. 5 + 6

1. 0 + 2	**2.** 7 + 7	**3.** 2 + 1	**4.** 4 + 10	**5.** 1 + 6
6. 4 + 4	**7.** 8 + 4	**8.** 8 + 5	**9.** 7 + 4	**10.** 7 + 5
11. 6 + 10	**12.** 7 + 5	**13.** 10 + 2	**14.** 4 + 0	**15.** 3 + 0
16. 5 + 6	**17.** 0 + 4	**18.** 10 + 7	**19.** 5 + 1	**20.** 6 + 6
21. 5 + 10	**22.** 6 + 5	**23.** 7 + 4	**24.** 9 + 7	**25.** 6 + 4
26. 1 + 2	**27.** 4 + 3	**28.** 2 + 8	**29.** 9 + 8	**30.** 7 + 3
31. 5 + 10	**32.** 9 + 6	**33.** 8 + 0	**34.** 8 + 10	**35.** 8 + 0
36. 3 + 5	**37.** 2 + 6	**38.** 6 + 2	**39.** 2 + 9	**40.** 10 + 3
41. 9 + 3	**42.** 3 + 10	**43.** 3 + 3	**44.** 6 + 7	**45.** 9 + 8

1. 5 + 5	2. 0 + 1	3. 0 + 2	4. 1 + 0	5. 8 + 7
6. 8 + 4	7. 9 + 0	8. 10 + 4	9. 1 + 10	10. 6 + 5
11. 2 + 0	12. 9 + 3	13. 3 + 5	14. 2 + 6	15. 7 + 4
16. 5 + 2	17. 8 + 6	18. 5 + 1	19. 8 + 2	20. 5 + 6
21. 4 + 8	22. 0 + 1	23. 5 + 0	24. 5 + 4	25. 10 + 8
26. 0 + 0	27. 5 + 1	28. 1 + 2	29. 1 + 10	30. 6 + 10
31. 1 + 0	32. 4 + 10	33. 4 + 8	34. 5 + 5	35. 3 + 7
36. 0 + 5	37. 4 + 0	38. 6 + 7	39. 5 + 0	40. 7 + 0
41. 8 + 7	42. 9 + 9	43. 4 + 8	44. 8 + 1	45. 7 + 7

1. 5 + 0	2. 9 + 6	3. 4 + 7	4. 3 + 10	5. 1 + 8
6. 3 + 1	7. 6 + 2	8. 1 + 2	9. 5 + 1	10. 4 + 4
11. 0 + 9	12. 10 + 0	13. 6 + 7	14. 5 + 4	15. 4 + 10
16. 10 + 10	17. 1 + 3	18. 3 + 6	19. 4 + 10	20. 7 + 5
21. 2 + 10	22. 6 + 0	23. 5 + 10	24. 3 + 6	25. 4 + 10
26. 9 + 4	27. 7 + 10	28. 9 + 10	29. 4 + 8	30. 9 + 10
31. 4 + 9	32. 6 + 4	33. 1 + 8	34. 6 + 6	35. 3 + 2
36. 5 + 9	37. 3 + 8	38. 7 + 8	39. 6 + 1	40. 10 + 7
41. 6 + 2	42. 1 + 3	43. 7 + 7	44. 5 + 1	45. 3 + 8

1.	7 + 6	2.	3 + 0	3.	0 + 6	4.	5 + 3	5.	4 + 8
6.	8 + 3	7.	6 + 7	8.	3 + 2	9.	8 + 9	10.	5 + 8
11.	7 + 9	12.	7 + 10	13.	10 + 9	14.	2 + 10	15.	2 + 10
16.	6 + 8	17.	2 + 1	18.	8 + 3	19.	8 + 10	20.	6 + 3
21.	0 + 0	22.	4 + 7	23.	4 + 8	24.	9 + 8	25.	2 + 10
26.	8 + 8	27.	7 + 7	28.	9 + 4	29.	9 + 5	30.	2 + 9
31.	3 + 9	32.	9 + 9	33.	5 + 4	34.	6 + 0	35.	3 + 5
36.	7 + 6	37.	6 + 1	38.	10 + 8	39.	3 + 5	40.	3 + 8
41.	3 + 6	42.	9 + 7	43.	3 + 2	44.	8 + 10	45.	9 + 8

1. 6 + 2	2. 8 + 5	3. 3 + 6	4. 0 + 6	5. 5 + 2
6. 7 + 5	7. 10 + 4	8. 7 + 3	9. 3 + 0	10. 8 + 7
11. 5 + 4	12. 1 + 4	13. 8 + 5	14. 7 + 4	15. 6 + 10
16. 6 + 9	17. 2 + 8	18. 9 + 10	19. 2 + 10	20. 2 + 2
21. 6 + 10	22. 9 + 7	23. 3 + 5	24. 10 + 8	25. 3 + 4
26. 5 + 9	27. 2 + 5	28. 10 + 10	29. 9 + 9	30. 3 + 10
31. 10 + 4	32. 10 + 3	33. 3 + 4	34. 3 + 9	35. 9 + 10
36. 6 + 7	37. 4 + 5	38. 3 + 2	39. 1 + 6	40. 9 + 2
41. 8 + 7	42. 8 + 9	43. 3 + 9	44. 0 + 6	45. 3 + 8

1. 5 + 7	2. 3 + 7	3. 0 + 0	4. 1 + 6	5. 8 + 0
6. 9 + 6	7. 8 + 5	8. 7 + 8	9. 9 + 10	10. 9 + 3
11. 5 + 10	12. 1 + 6	13. 8 + 9	14. 1 + 3	15. 3 + 8
16. 3 + 10	17. 8 + 10	18. 2 + 8	19. 8 + 7	20. 9 + 7
21. 4 + 8	22. 9 + 2	23. 8 + 0	24. 8 + 3	25. 8 + 10
26. 4 + 6	27. 10 + 1	28. 1 + 7	29. 8 + 6	30. 10 + 8
31. 10 + 1	32. 9 + 10	33. 8 + 6	34. 3 + 1	35. 10 + 7
36. 0 + 1	37. 0 + 3	38. 0 + 5	39. 3 + 10	40. 10 + 0
41. 10 + 2	42. 2 + 9	43. 4 + 6	44. 10 + 4	45. 7 + 6

1. 10 + 4	**2.** 8 + 3	**3.** 8 + 8	**4.** 2 + 0	**5.** 9 + 4
6. 6 + 2	**7.** 5 + 10	**8.** 9 + 0	**9.** 3 + 2	**10.** 3 + 5
11. 3 + 5	**12.** 0 + 6	**13.** 6 + 5	**14.** 5 + 8	**15.** 5 + 1
16. 10 + 0	**17.** 0 + 8	**18.** 2 + 10	**19.** 6 + 9	**20.** 7 + 8
21. 3 + 9	**22.** 8 + 1	**23.** 9 + 1	**24.** 9 + 3	**25.** 1 + 3
26. 7 + 4	**27.** 5 + 4	**28.** 8 + 10	**29.** 7 + 6	**30.** 10 + 5
31. 0 + 3	**32.** 5 + 1	**33.** 1 + 1	**34.** 0 + 6	**35.** 0 + 8
36. 5 + 2	**37.** 5 + 4	**38.** 9 + 0	**39.** 9 + 4	**40.** 7 + 4
41. 7 + 4	**42.** 10 + 9	**43.** 8 + 7	**44.** 3 + 1	**45.** 9 + 0

1. 7 + 4	2. 5 + 0	3. 4 + 6	4. 9 + 6	5. 8 + 10
6. 3 + 7	7. 9 + 6	8. 10 + 0	9. 3 + 9	10. 8 + 7
11. 4 + 5	12. 0 + 6	13. 9 + 8	14. 3 + 6	15. 4 + 5
16. 4 + 9	17. 5 + 7	18. 1 + 9	19. 3 + 10	20. 5 + 8
21. 5 + 10	22. 2 + 9	23. 2 + 2	24. 2 + 2	25. 5 + 2
26. 10 + 9	27. 5 + 0	28. 1 + 9	29. 1 + 8	30. 9 + 1
31. 9 + 3	32. 10 + 1	33. 9 + 10	34. 7 + 9	35. 6 + 5
36. 10 + 7	37. 6 + 6	38. 8 + 4	39. 9 + 0	40. 6 + 10
41. 2 + 5	42. 6 + 0	43. 10 + 10	44. 6 + 8	45. 4 + 4

1. 5 + 9	2. 8 + 10	3. 9 + 6	4. 8 + 5	5. 3 + 5
6. 9 + 4	7. 0 + 9	8. 4 + 8	9. 5 + 9	10. 7 + 1
11. 2 + 2	12. 5 + 8	13. 10 + 6	14. 9 + 9	15. 10 + 9
16. 4 + 0	17. 0 + 6	18. 9 + 9	19. 5 + 6	20. 7 + 6
21. 7 + 5	22. 4 + 6	23. 2 + 7	24. 4 + 2	25. 6 + 9
26. 9 + 2	27. 1 + 7	28. 7 + 6	29. 9 + 5	30. 6 + 5
31. 8 + 6	32. 3 + 5	33. 7 + 0	34. 1 + 1	35. 1 + 5
36. 7 + 9	37. 4 + 6	38. 7 + 7	39. 1 + 5	40. 5 + 4
41. 9 + 8	42. 7 + 6	43. 7 + 5	44. 7 + 6	45. 10 + 4

1. 8
   + 9
   _____

2. 1
   + 4
   _____

3. 6
   + 9
   _____

4. 5
   + 5
   _____

5. 9
   + 2
   _____

6. 6
   + 0
   _____

7. 4
   + 0
   _____

8. 7
   + 5
   _____

9. 9
   + 0
   _____

10. 5
    + 9
    _____

11. 6
    + 9
    _____

12. 1
    + 6
    _____

13. 2
    + 10
    _____

14. 7
    + 6
    _____

15. 3
    + 8
    _____

16. 3
    + 1
    _____

17. 0
    + 1
    _____

18. 8
    + 2
    _____

19. 0
    + 4
    _____

20. 3
    + 9
    _____

21. 8
    + 10
    _____

22. 2
    + 5
    _____

23. 9
    + 2
    _____

24. 4
    + 10
    _____

25. 6
    + 9
    _____

26. 1
    + 7
    _____

27. 6
    + 6
    _____

28. 8
    + 0
    _____

29. 8
    + 9
    _____

30. 10
    + 10
    _____

31. 0
    + 3
    _____

32. 10
    + 2
    _____

33. 8
    + 3
    _____

34. 2
    + 10
    _____

35. 5
    + 6
    _____

36. 9
    + 2
    _____

37. 6
    + 4
    _____

38. 6
    + 0
    _____

39. 5
    + 4
    _____

40. 3
    + 1
    _____

41. 1
    + 2
    _____

42. 4
    + 10
    _____

43. 10
    + 9
    _____

44. 2
    + 8
    _____

45. 9
    + 8
    _____

1. 1
+ 0

2. 7
+ 2

3. 4
+ 2

4. 3
+ 6

5. 3
+ 5

6. 3
+ 3

7. 3
+ 1

8. 0
+ 9

9. 6
+ 5

10. 7
+ 8

11. 7
+ 4

12. 4
+ 9

13. 8
+ 4

14. 6
+ 8

15. 8
+ 2

16. 7
+ 9

17. 1
+ 4

18. 2
+ 6

19. 8
+ 9

20. 9
+ 9

21. 6
+ 5

22. 5
+ 10

23. 5
+ 5

24. 8
+ 0

25. 2
+ 2

26. 1
+ 3

27. 2
+ 3

28. 8
+ 7

29. 4
+ 10

30. 0
+ 0

31. 10
+ 2

32. 2
+ 1

33. 10
+ 1

34. 4
+ 5

35. 8
+ 7

36. 9
+ 9

37. 0
+ 9

38. 8
+ 1

39. 8
+ 6

40. 3
+ 5

41. 5
+ 8

42. 8
+ 1

43. 3
+ 1

44. 6
+ 5

45. 5
+ 1

1. 10 + 1	**2.** 0 + 0	**3.** 4 + 9	**4.** 1 + 7	**5.** 0 + 8
6. 0 + 4	**7.** 8 + 3	**8.** 9 + 6	**9.** 8 + 10	**10.** 0 + 10
11. 2 + 5	**12.** 0 + 4	**13.** 1 + 4	**14.** 5 + 1	**15.** 7 + 8
16. 5 + 10	**17.** 3 + 3	**18.** 9 + 10	**19.** 6 + 9	**20.** 7 + 10
21. 10 + 0	**22.** 4 + 8	**23.** 7 + 6	**24.** 2 + 4	**25.** 7 + 1
26. 1 + 8	**27.** 10 + 2	**28.** 10 + 7	**29.** 1 + 8	**30.** 2 + 1
31. 4 + 3	**32.** 7 + 2	**33.** 1 + 8	**34.** 9 + 3	**35.** 4 + 8
36. 0 + 3	**37.** 5 + 0	**38.** 8 + 8	**39.** 6 + 1	**40.** 4 + 0
41. 3 + 8	**42.** 10 + 7	**43.** 2 + 1	**44.** 9 + 4	**45.** 10 + 1

1. 5 + 10	**2.** 5 + 5	**3.** 1 + 9	**4.** 6 + 3	**5.** 4 + 9
6. 4 + 9	**7.** 6 + 7	**8.** 6 + 4	**9.** 2 + 3	**10.** 3 + 3
11. 3 + 4	**12.** 10 + 10	**13.** 5 + 6	**14.** 0 + 9	**15.** 8 + 0
16. 7 + 10	**17.** 3 + 4	**18.** 6 + 1	**19.** 0 + 6	**20.** 7 + 1
21. 0 + 8	**22.** 6 + 1	**23.** 9 + 10	**24.** 3 + 9	**25.** 10 + 7
26. 1 + 7	**27.** 0 + 7	**28.** 7 + 1	**29.** 7 + 2	**30.** 3 + 2
31. 2 + 4	**32.** 1 + 7	**33.** 10 + 1	**34.** 0 + 0	**35.** 7 + 7
36. 8 + 3	**37.** 3 + 5	**38.** 3 + 1	**39.** 10 + 0	**40.** 6 + 10
41. 6 + 8	**42.** 10 + 4	**43.** 2 + 10	**44.** 2 + 10	**45.** 4 + 9

1. 6 + 6	2. 7 + 7	3. 4 + 4	4. 6 + 5	5. 0 + 7
6. 3 + 10	7. 0 + 4	8. 1 + 10	9. 8 + 7	10. 1 + 8
11. 6 + 10	12. 5 + 1	13. 8 + 6	14. 3 + 6	15. 7 + 7
16. 9 + 8	17. 4 + 2	18. 3 + 0	19. 8 + 1	20. 7 + 3
21. 7 + 8	22. 1 + 4	23. 0 + 3	24. 10 + 2	25. 9 + 6
26. 0 + 9	27. 8 + 3	28. 1 + 7	29. 5 + 7	30. 4 + 4
31. 4 + 3	32. 1 + 7	33. 0 + 7	34. 4 + 6	35. 2 + 8
36. 2 + 6	37. 1 + 8	38. 0 + 9	39. 5 + 2	40. 3 + 5
41. 8 + 4	42. 1 + 0	43. 8 + 3	44. 0 + 4	45. 10 + 3

1.   9
 + 5

2.   8
 + 10

3.   4
 + 1

4.   9
 + 8

5.   3
 + 3

6.   0
 + 1

7.   7
 + 5

8.   2
 + 10

9.   4
 + 2

10.   8
 + 4

11.   3
 + 10

12.   1
 + 0

13.   8
 + 2

14.   7
 + 3

15.   0
 + 3

16.   10
 + 0

17.   8
 + 3

18.   4
 + 7

19.   0
 + 3

20.   9
 + 3

21.   0
 + 7

22.   9
 + 6

23.   2
 + 9

24.   1
 + 2

25.   1
 + 7

26.   1
 + 8

27.   7
 + 1

28.   4
 + 5

29.   10
 + 8

30.   9
 + 4

31.   9
 + 9

32.   5
 + 7

33.   0
 + 3

34.   5
 + 10

35.   9
 + 0

36.   2
 + 9

37.   0
 + 9

38.   6
 + 3

39.   3
 + 0

40.   8
 + 0

41.   10
 + 7

42.   8
 + 7

43.   3
 + 4

44.   0
 + 4

45.   8
 + 7

1. 2 + 7	2. 8 + 7	3. 6 + 4	4. 3 + 6	5. 9 + 10
6. 5 + 7	7. 0 + 2	8. 1 + 0	9. 6 + 2	10. 10 + 10
11. 10 + 8	12. 9 + 10	13. 5 + 9	14. 9 + 3	15. 9 + 8
16. 5 + 9	17. 2 + 10	18. 4 + 7	19. 3 + 3	20. 7 + 5
21. 0 + 0	22. 7 + 9	23. 1 + 5	24. 3 + 10	25. 9 + 6
26. 2 + 0	27. 10 + 9	28. 6 + 5	29. 9 + 2	30. 4 + 6
31. 1 + 7	32. 5 + 1	33. 2 + 6	34. 6 + 7	35. 8 + 5
36. 0 + 7	37. 0 + 5	38. 10 + 7	39. 3 + 4	40. 3 + 0
41. 9 + 4	42. 8 + 10	43. 2 + 4	44. 9 + 7	45. 9 + 5

1. 0 + 5	2. 7 + 0	3. 4 + 6	4. 1 + 7	5. 4 + 6
6. 5 + 7	7. 3 + 8	8. 6 + 7	9. 5 + 1	10. 9 + 1
11. 0 + 6	12. 0 + 5	13. 6 + 10	14. 9 + 10	15. 9 + 7
16. 3 + 10	17. 10 + 2	18. 9 + 8	19. 5 + 8	20. 10 + 2
21. 1 + 9	22. 7 + 2	23. 5 + 5	24. 2 + 6	25. 1 + 4
26. 2 + 3	27. 7 + 2	28. 2 + 5	29. 3 + 6	30. 8 + 9
31. 9 + 1	32. 9 + 0	33. 1 + 6	34. 4 + 1	35. 7 + 6
36. 3 + 9	37. 4 + 10	38. 5 + 1	39. 3 + 5	40. 9 + 10
41. 10 + 7	42. 10 + 3	43. 9 + 9	44. 0 + 8	45. 2 + 9

Name_____ Date _____ Score _____

1. 2
  + 9
  ———

2. 3
  + 1
  ———

3. 10
  + 0
  ———

4. 5
  + 1
  ———

5. 2
  + 7
  ———

6. 4
  + 10
  ———

7. 3
  + 10
  ———

8. 6
  + 4
  ———

9. 2
  + 2
  ———

10. 7
  + 9
  ———

11. 4
  + 0
  ———

12. 3
  + 6
  ———

13. 6
  + 10
  ———

14. 9
  + 8
  ———

15. 7
  + 8
  ———

16. 0
  + 10
  ———

17. 6
  + 0
  ———

18. 7
  + 1
  ———

19. 9
  + 0
  ———

20. 8
  + 0
  ———

21. 5
  + 0
  ———

22. 0
  + 7
  ———

23. 2
  + 5
  ———

24. 6
  + 9
  ———

25. 4
  + 6
  ———

26. 3
  + 8
  ———

27. 7
  + 5
  ———

28. 4
  + 0
  ———

29. 6
  + 1
  ———

30. 3
  + 3
  ———

31. 10
  + 6
  ———

32. 1
  + 6
  ———

33. 1
  + 0
  ———

34. 1
  + 0
  ———

35. 6
  + 5
  ———

36. 9
  + 10
  ———

37. 9
  + 9
  ———

38. 8
  + 6
  ———

39. 3
  + 9
  ———

40. 0
  + 1
  ———

41. 5
  + 10
  ———

42. 4
  + 2
  ———

43. 1
  + 10
  ———

44. 7
  + 3
  ———

45. 1
  + 1
  ———

1. 10 + 8	2. 3 + 2	3. 6 + 9	4. 9 + 6	5. 7 + 7
6. 9 + 7	7. 8 + 7	8. 7 + 5	9. 3 + 10	10. 6 + 2
11. 9 + 3	12. 1 + 7	13. 10 + 9	14. 9 + 2	15. 0 + 6
16. 4 + 7	17. 4 + 4	18. 2 + 2	19. 0 + 9	20. 6 + 8
21. 2 + 3	22. 8 + 0	23. 7 + 9	24. 5 + 10	25. 6 + 9
26. 0 + 4	27. 4 + 2	28. 9 + 10	29. 4 + 10	30. 9 + 5
31. 7 + 3	32. 5 + 0	33. 1 + 6	34. 2 + 1	35. 5 + 5
36. 1 + 3	37. 9 + 10	38. 5 + 3	39. 7 + 4	40. 9 + 7
41. 3 + 7	42. 6 + 0	43. 10 + 3	44. 10 + 8	45. 8 + 10

1. 0
   + 4
   _____

2. 2
   + 2
   _____

3. 7
   + 1
   _____

4. 9
   + 5
   _____

5. 2
   + 4
   _____

6. 3
   + 4
   _____

7. 0
   + 3
   _____

8. 4
   + 6
   _____

9. 9
   + 5
   _____

10. 3
    + 9
    _____

11. 4
    + 5
    _____

12. 8
    + 7
    _____

13. 6
    + 6
    _____

14. 5
    + 5
    _____

15. 5
    + 6
    _____

16. 5
    + 7
    _____

17. 7
    + 4
    _____

18. 9
    + 1
    _____

19. 6
    + 2
    _____

20. 6
    + 5
    _____

21. 8
    + 4
    _____

22. 8
    + 6
    _____

23. 9
    + 1
    _____

24. 6
    + 3
    _____

25. 8
    + 10
    _____

26. 9
    + 8
    _____

27. 3
    + 1
    _____

28. 7
    + 7
    _____

29. 2
    + 3
    _____

30. 6
    + 0
    _____

31. 2
    + 0
    _____

32. 6
    + 2
    _____

33. 9
    + 10
    _____

34. 4
    + 4
    _____

35. 5
    + 2
    _____

36. 7
    + 10
    _____

37. 4
    + 7
    _____

38. 2
    + 2
    _____

39. 0
    + 2
    _____

40. 5
    + 3
    _____

41. 5
    + 7
    _____

42. 3
    + 7
    _____

43. 2
    + 6
    _____

44. 5
    + 6
    _____

45. 3
    + 7
    _____

1. 10 + 1	**2.** 4 + 6	**3.** 9 + 4	**4.** 3 + 10	**5.** 7 + 6
6. 1 + 9	**7.** 0 + 7	**8.** 9 + 5	**9.** 6 + 1	**10.** 2 + 10
11. 6 + 3	**12.** 5 + 8	**13.** 6 + 4	**14.** 5 + 7	**15.** 1 + 9
16. 6 + 7	**17.** 2 + 9	**18.** 4 + 7	**19.** 5 + 5	**20.** 4 + 10
21. 3 + 9	**22.** 4 + 6	**23.** 9 + 1	**24.** 1 + 5	**25.** 5 + 3
26. 0 + 8	**27.** 4 + 7	**28.** 5 + 2	**29.** 10 + 1	**30.** 3 + 6
31. 1 + 6	**32.** 10 + 2	**33.** 0 + 6	**34.** 5 + 3	**35.** 9 + 4
36. 7 + 8	**37.** 3 + 9	**38.** 7 + 6	**39.** 10 + 7	**40.** 10 + 9
41. 7 + 8	**42.** 0 + 3	**43.** 9 + 4	**44.** 9 + 8	**45.** 1 + 0

1. 4
  + 5
  ————

2. 8
  + 5
  ————

3. 0
  + 1
  ————

4. 9
  + 8
  ————

5. 4
  + 8
  ————

6. 10
  + 2
  ————

7. 5
  + 1
  ————

8. 10
  + 10
  ————

9. 5
  + 0
  ————

10. 6
  + 2
  ————

11. 6
  + 1
  ————

12. 1
  + 10
  ————

13. 7
  + 10
  ————

14. 5
  + 8
  ————

15. 9
  + 6
  ————

16. 3
  + 4
  ————

17. 4
  + 6
  ————

18. 3
  + 6
  ————

19. 10
  + 8
  ————

20. 10
  + 8
  ————

21. 3
  + 9
  ————

22. 1
  + 0
  ————

23. 2
  + 3
  ————

24. 4
  + 10
  ————

25. 10
  + 7
  ————

26. 9
  + 2
  ————

27. 2
  + 5
  ————

28. 1
  + 10
  ————

29. 1
  + 10
  ————

30. 7
  + 1
  ————

31. 4
  + 4
  ————

32. 3
  + 10
  ————

33. 9
  + 4
  ————

34. 10
  + 8
  ————

35. 2
  + 4
  ————

36. 7
  + 4
  ————

37. 10
  + 8
  ————

38. 1
  + 4
  ————

39. 6
  + 8
  ————

40. 4
  + 0
  ————

41. 0
  + 4
  ————

42. 8
  + 9
  ————

43. 1
  + 4
  ————

44. 2
  + 9
  ————

45. 7
  + 3
  ————

If you enjoyed this book. Please check out
2nd Grade Homeschool Math Timed Test Subtraction